BUG BOOKS

Beetle

Revised and Updated

Karen Hartley, Chris Macro, and Philip Taylor

Heinemann
LIBRARY

www.heinemann.co.uk/library
Visit our website to find out more information about Heinemann Library books.

To order:
☎ Phone 44 (0) 1865 888066
🖹 Send a fax to 44 (0) 1865 314091
🖥 Visit the Heinemann Bookshop at www.heinemann.co.uk/library to browse our catalogue and order online.

First published in Great Britain by Heinemann Library, Halley Court, Jordan Hill, Oxford OX2 8EJ, part of Harcourt Education.

Heinemann is a registered trademark of Harcourt Education Ltd.

Editorial: Diyan Leake and Catherine Clarke
Design: Kimberly R. Miracle and
Cavedweller Studio
Illustrations: Alan Fraser at Pennant Illustration
Picture Research: Melissa Alison
Production: Alison Parsons

Originated by Dot Gradations Ltd
Printed and bound in China by South China Printing Company

ISBN 978 0 431 01979 6 (hardback)
12 11 10 09 08
10 9 8 7 6 5 4 3 2 1

ISBN 978 0 431 01985 7 (paperback)
12 11 10 09 08
10 9 8 7 6 5 4 3 2 1

British Library Cataloguing in Publication Data
Hartley, Karen
Beetle. - 2nd Edition. - (Bug Books)
595.7'6
A full catalogue record for this book is available from the British Library.

Acknowledgements
The publishers would like to thank the following for permission to reproduce photographs:
© Ardea London pp. 4 (Pascal Goetgheluck), 8 (Bob Gibbons), 24, 26 (J. L. Mason); © Bruce Coleman pp. 6 (Dr Frieder Sauer), 9 (Andrew Purcell), 21 (Jeff Foott), 23 (P. Kaya); © Bubbles (Steve Shot) p. 28; © Garden Matters p. 29; © Getty Images pp. 7 (Martin Ruegner), 13 (Hans Pfletschinger); © NHPA pp. 5 (G. J. Cambridge), 14 (John Shaw), 15 (Stephen Dalton), 16 (Stephen Dalton), 25 (Anthony Bannister); © Oxford Scientific Films pp. 10 (G. I. Bernard), 11 (G. I. Bernard), 12 (G. I. Bernard), 17 (Stephen Dalton), 18 (M. Deeble & V. Stone), 20 (Doug Allan), 22 (George K. Bryce), 27 (Satoshi Kuribayashi); © Photolibrary (Avril Watson) p. 19.

Cover photograph of a scarab beetle reproduced with permission of NaturePL (Barry Mansell).

Every effort has been made to contact copyright holders of any material reproduced in this book. Any omissions will be rectified in subsequent printings if notice is given to the publishers.

Contents

Some words are shown in bold, **like this**. You can find out what they mean by looking in the glossary.

What are beetles?

Beetles are **insects**. They have six legs and two pairs of wings.

tough wing

flying wing

Beetles have very hard skin. Two of their wings are very tough. They protect the **delicate** flying wings.

5

antenna

Beetles are usually black, brown, or green.
They have two **antennae** on their heads.

There are many different types of beetles. They can be different shapes and colours. **Ladybirds** are beetles.

How big are beetles?

Most beetles are about as big as your thumbnail. Some are very tiny. They are smaller than a dot made with a pencil.

The largest beetle is **called** the Goliath beetle. It can be **as large as** a man's fist.

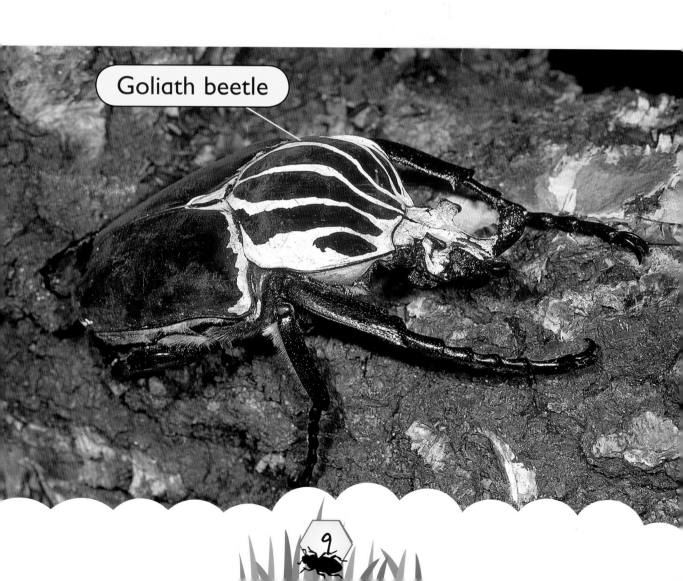

Goliath beetle

How are beetles born?

egg

Beetles are born in spring or autumn.
Most **female** beetles lay many eggs. They
lay them on the ground or on leaves.

10

larva

egg

Some beetles guard their eggs until they **hatch**. When the eggs hatch, **larvae** crawl out.

11

How do beetles grow?

Beetle **larvae** eat as fast as they can. When they have grown larger, they **moult**. The old skin breaks, the larva wriggles out, and a new larger skin grows.

The larva moults several times. Then it becomes a **pupa**. Inside the pupa it changes slowly and grows wings. When it **hatches** out it is an **adult**.

How do beetles move?

Some beetles have long thin legs. They can run fast. Others have shorter legs for digging. Some beetles have claws or sticky pads on their feet to help them climb.

Many beetles can fly but they do not fly for long. Some have wings that are not strong enough for flying.

What do beetles eat?

Many beetles eat other **insects**, worms, or snails. Some beetles eat plants or seeds.

beetle larva

tadpole

Beetle **larvae** can be very fierce. Water beetle larvae kill and eat **tadpoles**.

Which animals eat beetles?

Birds, lizards, and frogs eat beetles. In
some countries, people hunt large beetles
to make them into soup.

18

Some beetles make noises to frighten their enemies away. If the Bloody-nosed beetle is attacked, it squirts red liquid out of its mouth. This gives it time to escape.

Where do beetles live?

Beetles live in nearly every country in the world. Some types live in grasslands, in woodlands, or on the edges of rivers and streams.

Some beetles live on the seashore.
Others live near the tops of the highest
mountains. Some share the nests of
other **insects**.

How long do beetles live?

Some beetles live for less than a year.
Beetles sometimes **hibernate** during
the winter. They bury themselves in the
ground or in trees.

eggs

After the beetles lay their eggs
they die.

23

What do beetles do?

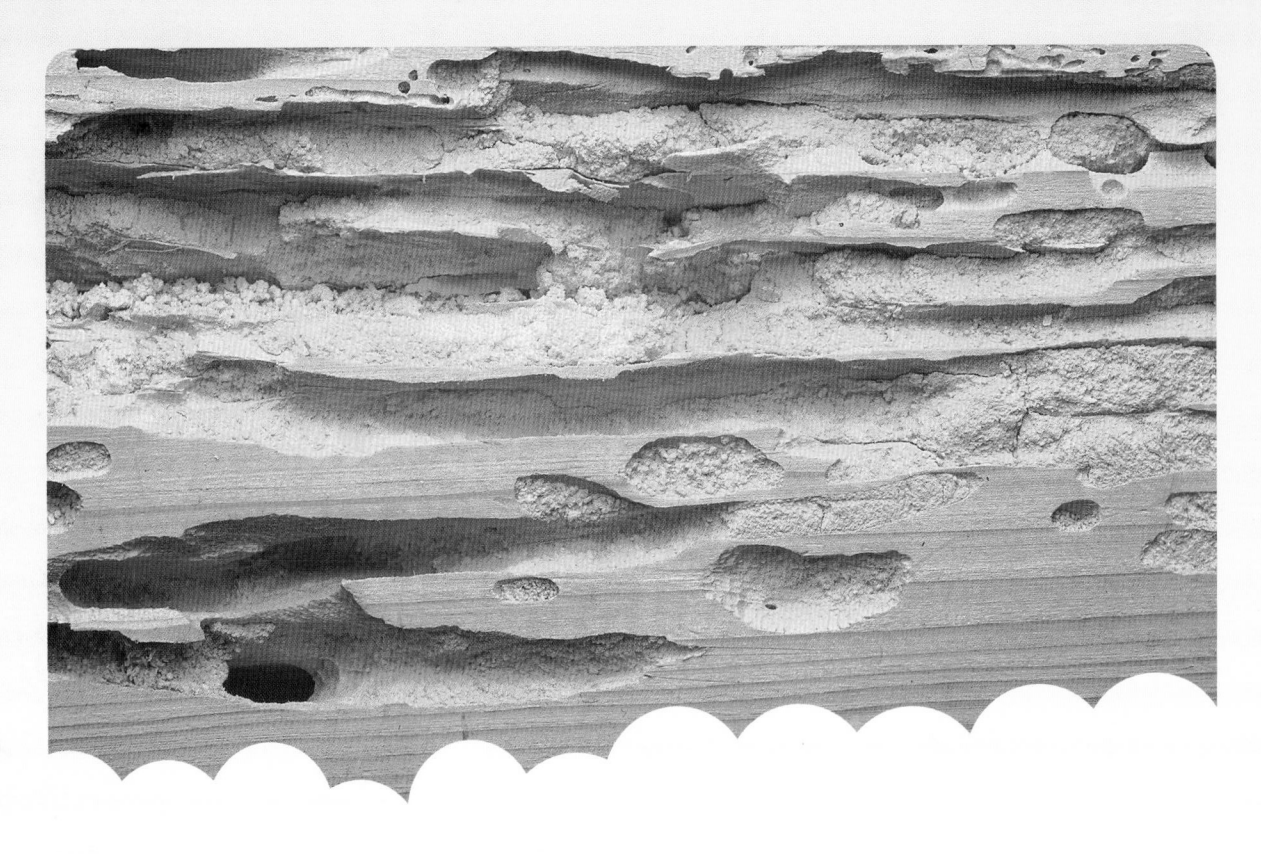

Many beetles spend their time under
stones or logs. It is damp and cool there.
Some live in houses. The **larvae** cause
damage by eating wood.

Dung beetles collect the dung from bigger animals. They roll it to make balls. Then they lay an egg in each ball.

How are beetles special?

There are more different types of beetles than any other type of animal. There are even beetles that live in ponds. They have legs like paddles.

Some beetles can glow in the dark.
Glow-worms and fireflies are really
types of beetles.

firefly

Thinking about beetles

Can you find some beetles? Turn over some stones and small logs to see if there are any underneath.

Turn stones and logs back again carefully when you have finished looking!

Why do you think they live there? What could happen to them if they were moved to a different place?

Bug map

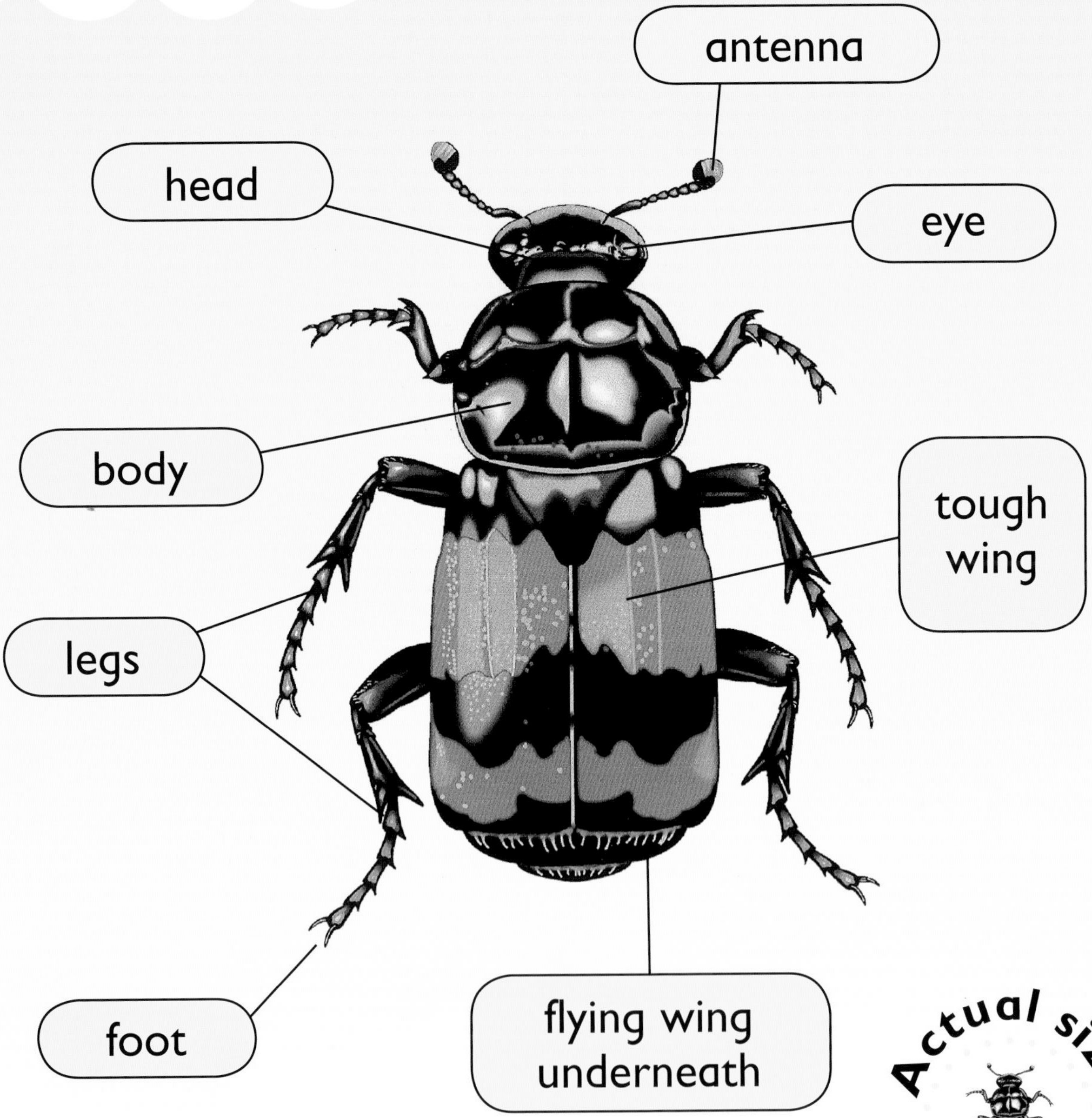

antenna

head

eye

body

tough wing

legs

foot

flying wing underneath

Actual size

Glossary

adult grown-up

antenna (more than one = antennae) long thin tube that sticks out from the head of an insect. Antennae can be used to smell, hear, feel, or sense direction.

delicate easy to damage or break

dung waste droppings that animals leave behind

female animal that can lay eggs or give birth to young. Women are females.

hatch break out of an egg

hibernate sleep through the winter

insect small creature with six legs and a body with three parts

ladybird type of beetle. They are usually red with black spots.

larva (more than one = larvae) baby insect that hatches from an egg

moult lose old skin. When an insect gets too big for its skin the old skin drops off and a new skin is underneath.

pupa (more than one = pupae) larva with a hard case around its body – before it turns into an adult

tadpole very young frog

Index

More books to read

First Library of Knowledge: World of Bugs, Nicholas Harris
    (Blackbirch Press, 2006)
Minibeasts: Beetles, Claire Llewellyn (Franklin Watts, 2004)
Minibeasts: Going on a Bug Hunt, Stewart Ross and Jim Pipe
    (Franklin Watts, 2006)